D0603214

Inventions That Shaped the World

The Light Bulb

J O H N   R.   M A T T H E W S

Franklin Watts
A Division of Scholastic Inc.
New York • Toronto • London • Auckland • Sydney
Mexico City • New Delhi • Hong Kong
Danbury, Connecticut

Photographs © 2005: Art Resource, NY/Scala/Museo Teatrale alla Scala, Milan, Italy: 18; Corbis Images: 11, 15 (Bettmann), 33 (Matthew B. Brady), 56 (Bojan Brecelj), 5 (Lester Lefkowitz), 23 (William Manning), 68 (Reuters), 59, 60 (Royalty-Free), cover top right, 44, 45, 57 (Schenectady Museum/Hall of Electrical History Foundation), 49; Culver Pictures: 39; Edison National Historic Site, National Park Service, U.S. Department of the Interior: 35; Getty Images: cover bottom right (Brian Hagiwara/Brand X Pictures), 8 (Hulton Archive), cover center (Photodisc Red); Hulton|Archive/Getty Images: 64; Mary Evans Picture Library: 17; Nick Romanenko: 26, 27, 29, 31, 36; North Wind Picture Archives: 22 (N. Carter), 14; Photo Researchers, NY: 42 (J-L Charmet/SPL), 61 (Raphael Macia), 7, 9 (SPL), 66 (Volker Steger/Siemens/SPL); Stock Montage, Inc.: cover left, 25, 51, 53; Superstock, Inc./Nora Scarlett: 69; The Art Archive/Picture Desk: 20 (Ara Collection Paris/Dagli Orti); The Image Works: 28 (ANA), 19 (Kent Meireis), 38 (Public Record Office/Topham-HIP), chapter openers, 6, 48 (Science Museum, London/Topham-HIP).

Light bulb illustration by Lucidity Information Design.

Cover design by Robert O'Brien and Kathleen Santini
Book production by Jeff Loppacker

Library of Congress Cataloging-in-Publication Data

Matthews, John R., 1937–
  The light bulb / John R. Matthews.
    p. cm. — (Inventions that shaped the world)
Includes bibliographical references and index.
    ISBN 0-531-12334-0 (lib. bdg.)   0-531-16721-6 (pbk.)
1. Light bulbs—Juvenile literature. I. Title. II. Series.
    TK4351.M38 2004
    621.32'6—dc22   2004001673

Contents

The Search for Electric Light

Think about all the light bulbs you use every day. You probably don't pay much attention to them. They are just there. There may be a light beside your bed. In fact, there are lights all over the home. There are light bulbs in the headlights of your family's car. Drivers couldn't see the road at night without them. If you use a flashlight to find a coin that rolled underneath your bed, it works because it has a

Without the light bulb this tunnel would be difficult to drive through. Light bulbs are used in car headlights, and they illuminate the inside of the tunnel, too.

5

light bulb in it. So does your refrigerator so you can see what's inside it. If you want to play baseball at night, there must be lights shining onto the field. There are light bulbs everywhere.

A Time of Great Inventions

If you like to read about history, you probably already know that the eighteenth and nineteenth centuries were times of great and wonderful inventions. It was an era known as the industrial revolution. This was a time when many new power-driven machines that helped people produce more goods were introduced. Steam engines powered machines in factories. The cotton gin processed fiber for spinning and weaving machines. The sewing machine replaced hand sewing.

An early steam locomotive hauls a train of coal wagons across a bridge.

The telegraph provided a means of instantaneous communication. Railroads began to connect all parts of the North American continent. The telephone would soon allow people to talk to each other across great distances. These were all great inventions.

You might not think of the light bulb as a "great" invention because it seems so simple. In a time when electricity was not well understood, however, it was not at all simple.

The Idea for an Electric Light

The idea for a light bulb emerged in the seventeenth century when scientists first began studying electricity seriously. An electric *arc light* was demonstrated by an English chemist,

A carbon arc lamp creates a continuous, bright glow as it lights the Place de la Concorde in Paris, France, for the first time.

Sir Humphry Davy, in 1809. The arc light produced light from an "arc" of electric current jumping from one wire to another. The intensely bright arc light was not a good replacement for the soft glow of lanterns and gaslights. The arc light was useful for streetlights that illuminated roadways and for light-houses that warned ships away from hazards, but it was not suitable for homes.

Gaslights and *kerosene* lamps and lanterns used in most nineteenth-century homes were fire hazards. They were hot in the summer and gave off unpleasant odors. A better lighting idea was needed.

By the late nineteenth century scientists were learning how to make and use electricity, necessary for any light bulb. *Generators*, sometimes called dynamos, for making electricity and batteries for

A cartoon from 1807 shows residents of England complaining about the effects of gas lighting.

storing it were developed for streetlamps that previously used arc lights. Then inventors began searching for an electric *incandescent* lamp, to be known as the light bulb.

This nineteenth-century steam-driven generator produced low-voltage electricity for local distribution.

The Search for an Incandescent Lamp

Thomas Alva Edison, the "Wizard of Menlo Park," had experimented with electric light as early as 1875. In 1878 he formally announced his intention to invent an electric light. He succeeded where others who tried had failed.

JOSEPH SWAN (1828–1914)

Throughout the nineteenth century inventors joined the race to develop an incandescent electric light. Thomas Edison was aware of the work of many of these inventors. Because inventors shared knowledge through patents, publications, and public demonstrations of their work, many of them provided Edison with information essential to the success of his own light bulb. An Englishman, Joseph Swan, demonstrated a workable light bulb months before Edison's bulb was ready.

Swan became a pharmacy apprentice at age thirteen. He soon developed an interest in the chemicals used in photography and joined a firm that manufactured a photographic chemical called collodion. While there in the 1840s, he began experiments that would lead to the invention of his light bulb.

He experimented with carbon filaments in the 1850s and 1860s but discovered that he needed a bulb with all the oxygen evacuated (a *vacuum*) to prevent the filament from producing soot or bursting into flame. When a vacuum pump became available in the 1870s that could create enough of a vacuum inside the bulb to prevent the filament from oxidizing, Swan resumed his experiments. He reported success to the Newcastle (England) Chemical Society in late 1878 and demonstrated a working lamp in February 1879.

In 1881 Swan formed a company in England, the Swan Electric Light Company, to market his bulb. Edison sued Swan for patent infringement

but lost the case in 1882. The financially more powerful Edison then formed a partnership with Swan in 1883. The new company was called The Edison and Swan United Company. Swan's important role in the development of the light bulb is often overlooked because Edison's bulb was part of a larger "invention," that of a complete lighting system, which included his electric distribution system.

Most nineteenth-century scientists and inventors knew that an electric incandescent lamp was possible. They knew electricity was capable of producing light that was superior to the light of candles, lanterns, and gaslights then in use. They just didn't know how to do it.

In the long nineteenth-century contest to invent an incandescent lamp, Thomas Edison won with his light bulb.

THE EDISON TEAM

When Thomas Edison began experiments to develop his first light bulb, he employed a team of researchers to do much of the work. These assistants conducted many of the experiments. Edison directed and inspired them. He supervised the final experiments himself to assure the project's success.

Lighting Before Electricity

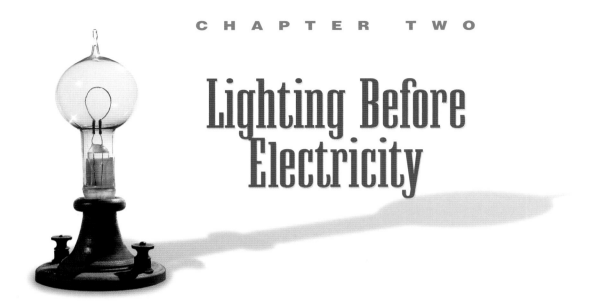

Imagine if you flipped the light switch on your lamp and nothing happened. You would first examine the bulb to see if it had burned out. You might change the light bulb. If the lamp still didn't work, you might check other lights in the house. If all the lights were out, you would start thinking about alternate sources of lighting. Where are the flashlights? Maybe there is a camping lantern in the garage. Surely there are candles somewhere in the house.

All this might set you to thinking about how nice it is to light your room by just flipping a switch. Most buildings are wired for electricity. They are also lit with electric light bulbs. Not long ago this would not have been true. In some countries even today, many homes and buildings still do not have electricity.

Life Before the Light Bulb

A little over a hundred years ago the electric light bulb had not yet been invented. How did people see in the dark? A look back in time can answer the question.

From the beginning of history until the eighteenth century, the only sources of nighttime light were candles, fireplaces, simple oil lamps, or cooking fires. Not much happened in public at night. All work and business was conducted during daylight hours.

A frontier father reads to his children by firelight.

Candles

One of the earliest forms of lighting was the candle. The material candles are made from has changed over time, but otherwise they remain the same. Ancient civilizations in Egypt and the Greek island of Crete used candles as early as 3000 B.C. The ancients also used *torch lights*, which were made by dipping rushes (grasslike plants) into melted fat. These torches burned very quickly, so they were not suitable to use for a long time.

Candles were used only in the houses of the rich, and perhaps in churches and palaces, until about the sixteenth

Workers complete all stages of the candle-making process as finished candles are sold in the storefront.

century. Candles were sold in markets. Some were made of beeswax or animal fat. Others were made from oil that came from the head cavity of sperm whales. These candles gave off a brighter light than other candles.

BETTER CANDLES IN THE NINETEENTH CENTURY

A French chemist, Michel-Eugène Chevreul (1786–1889), made an important discovery in about 1823. He found that tallow (animal fat), which was widely used for making candles, contained glycerin. He discovered that if he removed glycerin from tallow, he was left with a new substance, which he called *stearin*. Candles made from stearin are harder than tallow candles and burn longer.

After crude oil was discovered in the nineteenth century, a new form of wax, paraffin, was extracted from the oil in the refining process. Most candles today are made from paraffin. (The term "paraffin" is used in Great Britain to mean "kerosene.")

Lanterns

By the 1770s streets in Boston, Massachusetts, were lit by lanterns hanging from posts. Most lantern fuel was whale oil, the same oil used to make some candles. By the early

A lamplighter climbs up a ladder to light street lamps.

1800s lanterns were in use throughout the country. By the mid-nineteenth century a new fuel was used in lanterns. It was coal oil, which is similar to present-day kerosene.

Coal-oil lamps lit most homes in the nineteenth century. They were made of glass, porcelain, or metal. One end of a wick was placed in the oil. The other was lit to make the flame. These lamps were placed on tables. They had glass chimneys to control the amount of oxygen present around the wick, which controlled the rate at which it burned. They also had shades very much like our table lamps do.

In the 1800s lanterns along the stage and balconies lit theaters.

LIMELIGHT

"Limelight" describes something or someone in the center of attention. In the theater a limelight was a spotlight used to illuminate the stage. In 1816 a British engineer, Thomas Drummond, and his partner, Goldsworthy Gurney, discovered that heating a piece of lime in a cylinder until it glowed produced a bright light. When a lens was placed over the cylinder, it focused a spot of light onto the stage. It was probably first used in a theater in 1837. By 1860 its use was widespread.

The widespread use of lanterns and lamps allowed more nighttime activities. People could read in the evenings. They could invite friends to visit after dark. Public buildings could be used at night. Theater managers were especially interested in improving lighting technology. People preferred to attend theaters at night. Stages could be lit with footlights, which were lanterns placed along the apron (edge).

Mantles

Flat wicks in lamps and lanterns were replaced by mantles in the late 1800s. Mantles were small gauze cylinders that were treated with a chemical. The mantle glowed when heated and put out a bright light. Mantles are still found in lanterns and lamps used by campers.

Kerosene lamps and lanterns are still used in less developed countries and in some rural areas that are without

Mantles replaced flat wicks in the late 1800s. Mantles glow brightly when heated.

electricity. You may find such lamps somewhere in your own home that could be used in case of an electrical failure.

The Gaslight Era

Gaslight was another form of lighting used in the nineteenth century. Its light was similar to that of lanterns. Gaslight fixtures usually hung from ceilings or walls. Gas was carried through pipes to the fixture and burned to produce light. Gas was first used for lighting in 1792 by William Murdock in Cornwall, England. He learned how to extract gas from coal. Murdock installed gas lighting in his home.

The word "gas" is sometimes used as a short form of the word "gasoline," the fuel we burn in our cars. The gas used as fuel for gaslights, however, was not gasoline.

MANTLE PRESSURE LAMP

Gaslights were permanently fixed to either a ceiling or a wall. They could not be moved from room to room or to a table. That was because their fuel came from pipes through the wall or ceiling. The *pressure lamp* was a portable version of the gaslight. They were called pressure lamps because the fuel, usually kerosene, was pressurized by a built-in air pump. The pressurized fuel was forced upward toward the mantle. There it was vaporized and burned just as in a gaslight. Pressure lamps are still in use and can be bought in stores that sell camping equipment.

It was a vapor somewhat like the propane that is frequently used as fuel for backyard barbeque grills.

The first general use of gaslights was for lighting streets. Streets in a small area of London were lit with gaslights as early as 1807. Baltimore, Maryland, lit some of its streets with gaslights by 1817. Gaslights were more convenient to use than lamps or lanterns, which periodically had to be refueled.

Gas supplied a steady stream of fuel to create continuous light.

In 1825 the Chatham Garden Theater in New York became the first theater to use gas lighting throughout the entire building. The *New York Post* said the gaslights" shed a clear, soft light over the audience and stage." The White House in Washington, D.C., installed gaslights in 1848 while James Polk was president.

In order to use gas lighting, there had to be a gas supply. By the middle of the nineteenth century, private companies began supplying gas to homes and other buildings. The gas was piped from the gas plant through pipelines, the same as it is today. The first gas plants "manufactured" gas.

Natural gas is widely available. Here it travels through a winding pipeline in Alaska.

Manufactured gas was extracted from coal. Later in the nineteenth century a better form of gas was discovered. It was natural gas, found far beneath the ground.

Today natural gas is widely available. It is used for heating and cooking, not lighting. However, some people

23

have installed decorative gaslights in their front yards. These lights work in the same way as the nineteenth-century streetlights.

The Electric Light Bulb

Once electric lighting became available, people began switching from gaslights to electric lights. The development of a workable electric light bulb was slow because there were many things about electricity that were not yet well understood. For one thing, it was difficult to generate electricity. Once generated, it was difficult to store and to control. But the development of the primitive arc light in the early nineteenth century intrigued inventors. They knew that an incandescent, or glowing, light, was needed, not the blinding arc light. Thomas Alva Edison had joined the quest for a light bulb in 1878. His bulb would become the standard.

CHAPTER THREE

The Wizard of Menlo Park

Thomas Alva Edison was born February 11, 1847, in Milan, Ohio, the youngest of the seven children of Samuel and Nancy Edison. His mother was a former schoolteacher. His father at one time sold real estate. At another time he ran a grocery store. When Thomas was seven years old, the family moved to Port Huron, Michigan.

Thomas started school in Port Huron, but he didn't do well. His first teacher found him to be a difficult student. His mother decided to take him out

Thomas Alva Edison

of school and teach him at home. A hearing problem plagued Edison throughout his life; that may have been the reason his teachers found him to be a difficult student. Thomas developed an interest in science, mathematics, and literature. By age eleven his parents had introduced him to the local library. There he read classic literature, including Edward Gibbon's *Decline and Fall of the Roman Empire*. He also read works on science and mathematics. His self-directed learning set the course for his research method when he later embarked on life as an inventor.

Growing Up

Edison's learning outpaced his parents' ability to teach him. He read works by Isaac Newton, the eighteenth-century English scientist who first described the law of gravity. When Edison asked his parents to explain the ideas of Newton and other scientists, they were unable to do so. They hired a tutor to help him understand science. He began to learn how scientific knowledge progressed through experimentation.

Edison developed the habit of questioning whatever he read. He even questioned the writings of established and famous scientists. As a result he began to develop improvements to

The young Thomas Edison

existing technologies, such as the telegraph. He was also inspired to invent completely new technology. An example was his invention of the phonograph (record player), which was inspired by the telephone.

Early Work Experience

While Edison continued his studies, he also went to work. At age twelve he sold newspapers and snacks on a train. The train made a day trip from Port Huron to Detroit and

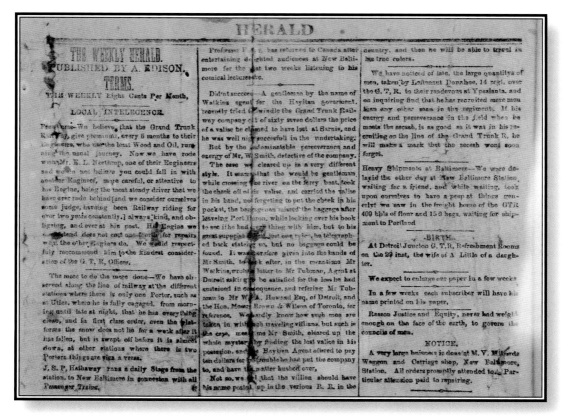

Edison's Weekly Herald

back again. Working around train stations, the curious newsboy gained access to the telegraph office. News was often sent between telegraph stations before it was published in newspapers. Edison took advantage of his access to the telegraph office to publish a newspaper, which he named the *Weekly Herald*.

In his later teens Edison learned to operate the telegraph machine. He worked as a telegraph operator in several different cities. These operators had to learn how to use Morse

A telegraph operator in a railroad station telegraph office sends a telegraph using Morse code while a client writes a message he would like to send.

EDISON AND THE
DUPLEX TELEGRAPH

1868 Edison left Port Huron for Boston to work as a telegrapher. There, a secondhand bookshop, he found a book by Michael Faraday, a pioneer of electrical research. By repeating the experiments that Faraday described, Edison learned the fundamentals of generating electricity. Faraday became his main inspiration. Edison confided to a friend, "I am now twenty-one. I may live to be fifty. Can I get as much done as he did? have got so much to do and life is so short that I am going to hustle."

And he did hustle. Only a year later he put an advertisement in a trade journal announcing that Thomas A. Edison "would hereafter devote his ll time to bringing out his inventions." The same ad offered his newly invented duplex telegraph, or double transmitter (below), for $400. The double transmitter was a telegraph that allowed two messages to be sent opposite directions at the same time on a single wire. Most of his early inventions would be improvements and variations on the telegraph.

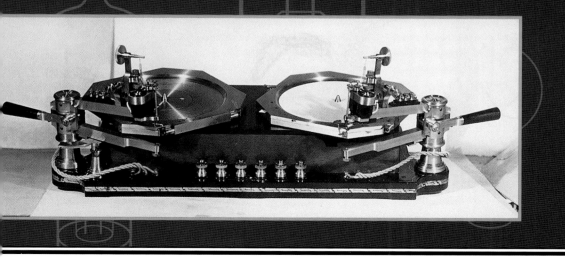

code, named for Samuel Morse, the inventor of the telegraph. Morse code used a combination of long and short marks, called dots and dashes, on a tape to represent letters of the alphabet. Later, the tape was eliminated and operators transcribed messages from the clicking sounds made by the telegraph. Messages could be sent over wires to many places across the country using Morse code.

Edison also worked for a clockmaker and in printing plants. Wherever he worked, he studied the equipment used for the jobs. He wasn't satisfied just knowing how to operate the machines. He wanted to know how they were put together and what their inventors were thinking as they assembled them.

Early Inventions

In 1868 Edison invented a vote recorder that used the telegraph. He was granted his first patent for that invention. A patent is an ownership right granted by the federal government. The patent gives the inventor the exclusive right to make, sell, or use his or her invention. Nobody wanted to buy Edison's voting machine, however.

The next year Edison made improvements to the stock ticker. Stock tickers printed prices from the stock exchange. Each stock ticker needed an operator to make it work. Edison's invention made the tickers work automatically, without operators. He named the device the Edison Universal Printer

Edison's stock ticker was used to receive telegraph messages and print them out on a strip of paper.

and sold the rights for $40,000, more than $500,000 in today's money.

At last he could start his own business and spend all his time inventing. He hired assistants and opened a workshop in Newark, New Jersey. There he often spent eighteen hours a day working on his inventions. He developed many electric devices in that shop, including a further improvement on the telegraph.

In 1871, when he was twenty-four, he met Mary Stilwell. She was sixteen and worked at his company. She became his first wife. They had a daughter, Marion, and two sons, Thomas Jr. and William.

Menlo Park Laboratory

During the five years he operated his workshop in Newark, he earned enough money to construct the first industrial research laboratory at Menlo Park, New Jersey. The laboratory opened in 1876. The first invention developed there was an improvement on the telephone. Alexander Graham Bell's telephone, invented in 1876, could operate over a range of only 2 to 3 miles (3.2 to 4.8 kilometers). Users had to shout into it to be heard. Edison's telephone could operate over a longer distance.

Inspired by the telephone, Edison invented the phonograph in 1877. The telephone worked by vibrating a thin membrane in tune with the voice as it spoke. The vibrating membrane, or diaphragm, reproduced a noise like that of the person speaking into the telephone. Edison was fascinated. He wondered if it would be possible to "preserve" those vibrations so they might be repeated over and over.

Thomas Edison with his first phonograph

Edison devised a diaphragm similar to the one in the telephone. He held one end of a needle to the surface of the diaphragm and the other end to the surface of a piece of wax paper. He then shouted "hello" into the diaphragm while dragging the wax paper underneath the needle. The needle was pulled along the grooves it had just made. The needle vibrated the diaphragm just as his voice had done. The vibrations reproduced Edison's shouted "hello."

Even though the experiment was very basic, it was sufficient to convince Edison that his phonograph was possible. He applied for a patent in 1877. By that time he had replaced the waxed paper with metal cylinders covered with tinfoil.

Edison postponed further development of the phonograph for several years. He wanted to move forward with his greatest invention: the incandescent lamp.

The Light Bulb

The idea for using electricity to generate lighting had been around for a long time. As we have seen, it was already possible to produce an arc light by creating an electric arc between two wires or carbon rods.

Edison's plan, which he adopted from other inventors before him, was to find a suitable filament. A filament is a wire that glows when electricity is passed through it. He needed to invent a filament that would not be broken or burned up by the electric current when heated. After a year of work and hundreds of trials, he developed a filament that burned for more than forty hours and used very little current. Edison's light bulb would lead to a whole new industry: the electric power distribution system.

Edison knew that if people were to use his light bulb, they needed a safe, reliable supply of electricity. He developed a detailed plan to supply electricity to homes and businesses. In 1881 he set up a complete electric supply system at his Menlo Park home and workshop to demonstrate how a distribution

The dynamo room at Edison's Pearl Street station generated electricity for homes and businesses in that area of New York City.

system could work. He later established a power station at Pearl Street in New York City to supply electricity to homes and businesses in that neighborhood.

Edison's Second Marriage

In 1884 Edison's wife Mary died of typhoid fever. He married his second wife, Mina Miller, in 1886. They had a daughter, Madeleine, and two sons, Charles and Theodore.

After his second marriage he bought Glenmont, a large country estate in West Orange, New Jersey. He moved his laboratory to Glenmont and remained there for forty-five years.

THE GLENMONT ESTATE

Edison bought Glenmont in January of 1886 as a wedding present for his new bride, Mina. By that time Edison was both rich and famous. The estate had been built for an executive who went into bankruptcy shortly after he took possession of it. Edison paid $123,000 for it. Edison said at the time, "To think it was possible to buy a place like this. . . . The idea fairly turned my head and I snapped it up."

The thirteen-acre (5.3 hectare) estate included a twenty-nine-room house, greenhouses, and other outbuildings. Edison spent little time in the beautiful house. He was too busy in his laboratory.

Mina loved the house and giving parties. On Christmas Day she would set up an elaborate table in the dining room for thirty guests. Edison, however, would often complain of a headache before one of Mina's parties and retire to his bedroom.

Glenmont is preserved as a part of the Edison National Historic Site and is now a museum open for public tours.

Edison's Motion Pictures

In 1888 Edison was inspired by Eadweard Muybridge, an English-born photographer, to develop motion pictures. In California Muybridge had set up a series of cameras to capture the motion of a running horse, a process called sequential photography. Each camera was tripped in rapid succession as the horse passed. That produced a series of pictures similar to the ones produced by modern movie cameras. Unfortunately, the method was so cumbersome that it had no practical use.

Edison took the idea and used it to develop the first motion-picture camera. His first camera was a cylinder that took about forty pictures per second. This device wasn't much more practical than Muybridge's method.

In 1889 the Eastman Company produced the first film that came in rolls made from a clear, pliable material called celluloid. Edison replaced his cylinder with the new celluloid film rolls. Prior to the use of celluloid, photographs were produced on glass negatives for later transfer to paper or were made directly on metal. Moving pictures made from these photographs were much too cumbersome to be practical. Celluloid, which resembles clear, pliable plastic, changed that. For the first time filmstrips could be hundreds of feet long. Edison and his assistant William Dickson used celluloid in their movie camera that was completed in 1890. Bendable film that unrolled from one spindle to another as

MOVING PICTURES WITH SOUND

The first motion pictures were not the projected images we are used to seeing. Instead, they were seen using a device Edison called a kinetoscope. The kinetoscope was a box with a small hole for viewing. The pictures "moved" when a crank was turned. In 1895 Edison experimented with a device he called a kinetophone, which was just a phonograph inside the kinetoscope. The two devices were connected with a belt so that sound was more or less synchronized with the moving picture.

The device was an interesting curiosity. People were happy to visit kinetoscope parlors once and pay a nickel to view the short movie, but customers eventually stopped coming. The invention of the *projector* revived interest in motion pictures. The projector, by showing moving pictures on a large screen, allowed many people to watch the pictures together (below) and generated a larger income.

it was exposed made longer films possible. The result, completed in 1890, was the first successful movie camera.

Edison's Long Career

For all of his life, Edison continued to invent. He made improvements on many already existing inventions. In 1900 he improved the electric storage battery, the battery used today in automobiles. In the 1920s he found alternate plant sources for producing rubber.

He patented more than one thousand inventions. Some of those inventions—the light bulb, the phonograph, and the motion-picture camera—gave rise to major industries that changed the way people lived.

Edison's first industrial research lab was nicknamed the "invention factory." Edison and his staff invented and improved many products there.

Today the motion picture industry employs thousands of people and generates billions of dollars in revenues. Likewise, thanks to Edison's phonograph, the recording industry employs thousands and generates billions of dollars. The economic impact of industries made possible by the invention of the light bulb is incalculable.

Edison often worked eighteen hours a day. He sometimes conducted dozens or even hundreds of experiments before he finally found one that worked. He often said genius consisted of 1 percent inspiration and 99 percent perspiration. The perspiration came from performing the dozens of experiments!

Before starting an invention project, Edison read all the available literature on the subject to avoid repeating experiments others had already conducted. He had a positive attitude about experiments. He said, "I have not failed. I've just found 10,000 ways that won't work."

Thomas Edison died on October 18, 1931, aged eighty-four years. He was buried at Glenmont, his New Jersey estate.

Inventing the Light Bulb

Edison conducted thousands of experiments before he produced a successful incandescent light bulb. He had three major obstacles to overcome in his quest. First, he had to find a long-lasting filament. Second, he needed to create a vacuum inside the bulb. To create a vacuum, he needed to remove as much air as possible without breaking the bulb. The vacuum prevented the filament from oxidizing, or catching fire. Last, he needed to design an electric distribution system.

Edison educated himself thoroughly about electricity. He knew all about Swan's carbonized paper filament. He knew about Davy's arc lights. His goal was the same as theirs—to develop a usable incandescent lamp that gave off bright, glowing light.

Electricity

As early as 1800 the Italian inventor Alessandro Volta made a primitive electric battery. Lots of inventors and scientists then began to have ideas about how electricity could be used to light streets, factories, and even homes. It wasn't until 1879 that Thomas Alva Edison was able to show the world how it could be done.

Alessandro Volta demonstrates his newly invented battery to Napolean.

Most scientists experimenting with electricity saw the potential for electric light, and some even managed to create bulbs. However, only Edison would make a satisfactory light bulb and develop an electric supply to make it work.

Nine years after Volta made his battery, Sir Humphry Davy, an English chemist, improved it. Davy discovered that if he passed a current between two carbon rods, then pulled the rods apart, an "arc" of current passed between the rods, creating an arc light. The date of this experiment is not certain but may have been as early as 1802. In 1809 he demonstrated his light to the Royal Institution of London. Davy then made what was perhaps the first electric light. The carbon glowed brightly—but very briefly. The light quickly depleted the batteries. Davy's light would remain a scientific curiosity.

Other scientists throughout the nineteenth century also contributed to the body of knowledge needed to develop a usable

EDISON'S LABORATORY

Edison's laboratory became a prototype for later industrial research laboratories operated by such large companies as General Electric. Edison's laboratory was organized so that either individuals or teams of assistants worked on specific parts of an invention. One assistant might be assigned to gather information about what other inventors were doing. Another might research patents or magazine articles relating to the invention. Some assistants had specialized knowledge or skills others lacked. Together, the teams represented

abilities greater than those of any one person. Edison's assistants deserve much credit for contributions to his inventions.

His assistant William Dickson may have contributed as much or more to the invention of the movie camera than Edison himself. Francis Upton, a mathematician, was hired by Edison to find out everything that was known about previous work on the light bulb. Nonetheless, there was never any doubt that in the end all the inventions were Edison's.

light bulb. None, however, can be called the *inventor* of the light bulb. The reason is that none was able to demonstrate how his invention could be useful to the public. Some of the bulbs used excessive amounts of energy; some burned out very quickly. None of the inventors followed through with ways to supply electricity to potential users of the light. Thomas Edison did.

The Vacuum Bulb

For his early experiments Edison used a simple air pump to create a vacuum within the bulbs. He searched for better ways. He learned of a pump invented in 1865 called the Sprengel mercury vacuum pump. He borrowed one and continued his experiments. The Sprengel pump created the vacuum he wanted.

A worker seals incandescent light bulbs.

The next problem was to devise a method to seal each bulb while it was still connected to the pump. This would prevent air from leaking into the bulb. He had glassblowers blow a bulb around the filament

45

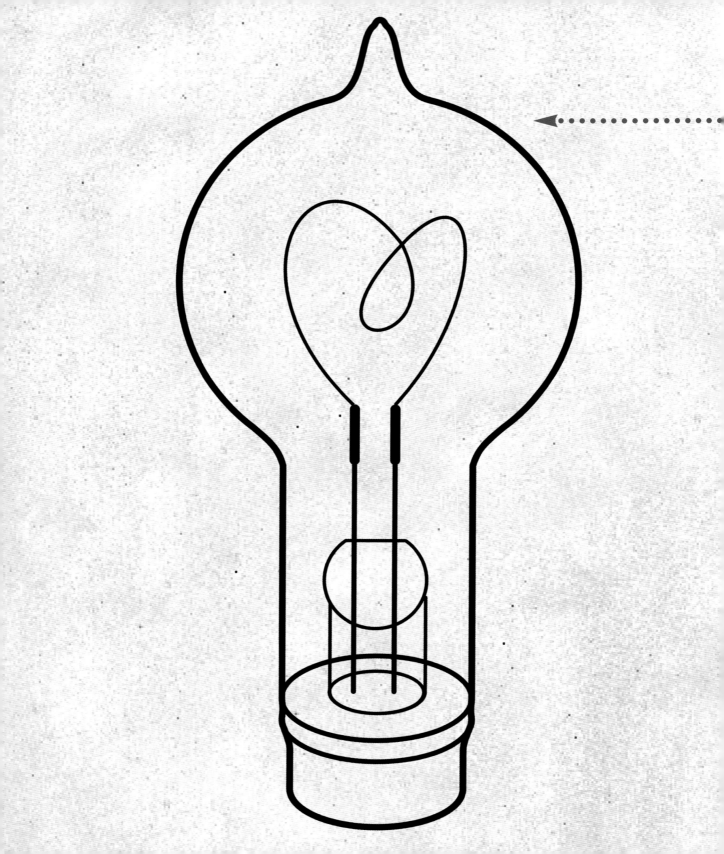

an early light bulb, probably from the 1890s. It
*…*ith present-day bulbs. It was about the same
*…*d its workings were similar. Both produce light
… the filament, causing it to glow. The earliest
*…*ssblowers shaping the bulb by hand; later, glass
… to produce more uniform shapes. The looped
*…*ustration is the bulb's filament. In Edison's day
*…*rbonized thread or bamboo. Today's bulb uses
filaments of very thin tungsten wire wound into coils that, when
stretched out, might be as long as 6 feet (1.8 meters). The filament is
attached to "leading-in wires" that electrify the filament and hold it in
place. The leading-in wires are held in place by the glass insulator at
the bulb's base.

You might wonder why such a simple device took almost a century
to develop. The answer is the filament. Edison had to find a metal or
other substance that would glow when heated but wouldn't easily break
or burn out. Edison conducted thousands of experiments before he found
a workable filament.

and seal it to the bulb's base while still connected to the
pump. By April of 1879 he was able to manufacture bulbs
with a satisfactory vacuum.

Search for a Filament

In Edison's first light bulb two wires rose out of the base.
Those wires were connected by the filament. When elec-
tricity flowed through the filament, it glowed, producing light.
Edison's first filaments were very delicate. They burned only

Edison's filament lamp had one loop of carbon that glowed when electricity flowed through it. The vacuum allowed the filament to become very hot without catching fire.

a few minutes before breaking. Edison needed to find a filament that would burn for a long time.

Although Edison didn't announce his search for a filament until 1878, he made some experiments long before then. In 1876 he began to experiment with carbonized paper. When he

Edison experiments with carbonized paper in his New Jersey laboratory.

passed an electric current through it, it glowed. After a few seconds, however, it disintegrated. He had a long way to go to find a workable filament. He tested many metals in his search, platinum and titanium among them. Platinum looked so promising that he filed a patent application for a platinum filament. He later abandoned that idea because platinum was too expensive. He also tested tungsten, the metal that is used today for filaments. But in the 1870s there was no method for forming tungsten into wire thin enough for a filament.

After many failures and near successes he returned to carbon. In one experiment he mixed powdered carbon with tar and rolled it out into a thin thread, and then tested it. It glowed for a long time before breaking.

Edison was now ready to think about ways to develop his electric light for widespread use. He would first tackle the problem of generating electricity to light the bulb. A method for distributing electricity to users of the light bulb would be the next project. These would prove to be the most difficult problems of all.

Edison wanted to prove that the light bulb could be used in homes. He dreamed that his bulb would replace gaslights, which were widely used in cities. Edison began to think about how he would build the power stations that would generate electricity for his lighting customers. He had to get the electricity from the power stations into each individual building.

Electric Distribution System

Edison would have to solve many problems to make his electric distribution system work. To overcome those problems, he needed lots of money. He found investors who were willing to back his light bulb project in return for a share of the profits to be earned by the invention. Edison and his investors formed a company in 1878 named the Edison Electric Light Company to provide Edison with the money he needed to perform his experiments. Several companies that Edison formed would later combine to become today's General Electric Company.

In 1880 Edison filed a patent application titled "System of Electrical Distribution." He described how each component, including the light bulb, that would provide lighting to

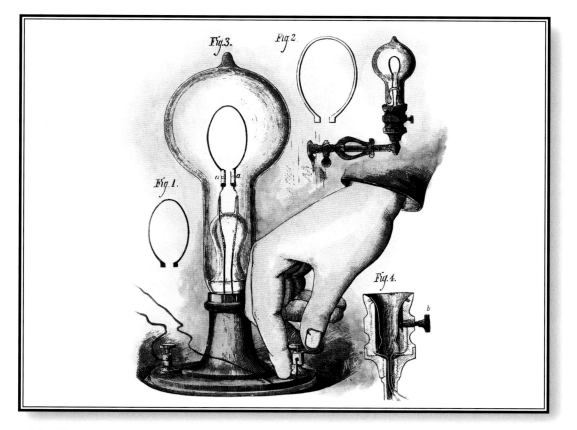

This illustration depicts Edison's electric lamp, the wiring, and the switch that turned the current on or off.

customers would be supplied. He formed a company in 1881, the Edison Machine Works, to manufacture the generators and other heavy equipment needed to supply electricity to customers. He contracted with another company to make switches, fuses, light fixtures, and sockets. For people wanting the new electric light, Edison companies would be able to supply a complete package from electric power to wiring to a supply of light bulbs.

For the first demonstration of his system, Edison chose a small area in downtown Manhattan that he designated as "First District" for supplying electric lighting to customers in the area. The district included both homes and factories. His plan called for burying the electric wiring beneath streets. His customers would be people who used gaslights in their homes or factories. He did a survey to determine how much gas each building in the area used. Part of Edison's sales strategy was to convince potential customers that his lighting system was cheaper than gas lighting.

Edison had to perfect other inventions before he could say his light bulb invention was complete. He needed to know how much electricity each household used so he could charge them for it. He invented the first electric meter. He needed centrally located power stations to supply electricity to each customer. The financial backers who formed many of Edison's companies provided money to build power stations and string electric wires through neighborhoods.

Thomas Edison's electric meter recorded the amount of electricity each customer used. The customer would be billed for the total amount used.

Edison thought of every detail needed to make his invention useful. Because his customers would no longer use their gaslights, he designed special bulbs that could be fitted into gaslight fixtures! Electric wires would be run through the gas pipes to the light fixtures. Table pressure lamps would be wired for the bulb and could be carried from room to room.

The companies Edison formed to promote the light bulb made sure that potential customers could purchase everything they needed to install electric lights in their homes and businesses. People began wiring their houses as soon as Edison's power companies ran wiring near their homes.

Nevertheless, competitors lost no time stringing electrical wiring throughout communities that did not have access to Edison's power stations. The Westinghouse Company became a major competitor for supplying electricity and speeded the electrification of America

At last, as customers began to wire their houses for electricity, Edison had succeeded in completing his most difficult and most important invention. Although over time other inventors would make improvements to the light bulb and to Edison's electric distribution system, its basic concept and uses remain unchanged.

The Electronic Era

The invention of the light bulb has changed the way we live our lives. No longer do we need to end our days at sunset. We can read or study after dark. We can shop in malls or eat in restaurants that are open all night. Factories can use their manufacturing facilities twenty-four hours a day, lowering production costs. Sporting events can be held at night, a time most convenient for many sports fans.

The colossal impact of Edison's invention goes well beyond the convenience provided by the light bulb. The light bulb brought the need for homes and businesses to be wired for electricity. The availability of electricity throughout the country made many other inventions possible. Many of those inventions used some kind of electric light. For example, lighting has always been important for theater performances.

Theaters were among the first businesses to adopt both gas lighting and electric lights. Theater spotlights once used lamps that burned lime for fuel (limelights). They then used gaslights, followed by arc lights. Spotlights use a lens in front of the light to focus either small lit spots or broad flood-lit areas on stage. Spotlights can even produce a round beam with a "hot," or bright, center and soft light around the edges.

A device that can dim lights, or slowly fade to darkness, was first used in theaters in 1933. Called a dimmer, it is often found in homes. It may be used to dim or brighten a chandelier hanging over a dining table, for example.

Another light sometimes used in theaters is the strobe light. It was developed in 1926 and is similar to the pulsating

Light shows are popular in dance clubs.

lights on top of police cars and ambulances. These lights rotate and provide an on-off series of beams or a series of different colors. When on-off strobes are aimed at moving people, their movements appear to rapidly stop, then start again. This produces a jerky stop-motion appearance. These lights were popular in 1960s-era discotheque nightclubs. They are often used in rock concert light shows.

UNDER THE LIGHTS

The first major league baseball game played at night was on May 24, 1935. The game was played at Crosley Field in Cincinnati, Ohio. The Cincinnati Reds beat the Philadelphia Phillies 2 to 1.

The lighting for the game was provided by 652 lamps of 1,500 watts each. The lamps were mounted on eight 130-foot towers at a cost of $50,000. The historic event was witnessed by more than twenty thousand baseball fans.

Neon Light

Many businesses use neon signs to attract the attention of customers. If you drive or walk along a busy commercial street, you can notice these signs several blocks away. Some may be flashing. You will see signs of many different colors. Neon itself produces just one color, red. Other colors are produced using other gases.

GLOWING NEON

Neon is a gas extracted from air. Georges Claude, a French chemist, displayed a neon lamp in 1910. The lamp worked by running an electrical current into a sealed glass tube filled with the gas. His lamp was later made into signs.

Neon signs first appeared in the United States in 1923. The first sign customer was a Packard car dealer in California. The sign read simply PACKARD. The new signs quickly gained in popularity.

It was soon discovered that using a different gas, argon, produced a blue light. When yet other elements or chemicals are added, such as mercury, many different colors can be created. Regardless of the gas used, all such signs are called neon.

Other Light Sources

Inventors are constantly finding new sources and imaginative uses for light. For example, in 1930 a German inventor, Johannes Ostermeir, patented the flashbulb. This bulb, used

A neon glow lights the Las Vegas night with its bright colors.

with cameras to illuminate objects being photographed, ignited a piece of foil within the bulb that shone brightly for a short moment. The flashbulb made it possible to photograph people indoors or in motion, such as at sporting events, resulting in some memorable photo journalism.

You can think of the picture tube in your TV or your computer monitor as relatives of light bulbs. Both use electric light to transmit their images. New flat-panel TVs and notebook computers use *liquid crystal display (LCD)* to create their images. LCDs began to be widely used in the 1990s and are also used to display the images in digital watches and clocks, microwave ovens, and dashboard displays in some newer vehicles.

If you look around your house, you may notice that some appliances have tiny lights to indicate that the appliance is either off or on. These lights are called *light emitting diodes (LEDs)*. LEDs are ideal for indicator lights because of their long life and low energy usage. The first LEDs, introduced in 1965, came in red only, but other colors—green, amber, blue, and white—were added later. A new kind of LED, the organic light emitting diode (OLED), was developed in the early 2000s. It is less costly to manufacture and uses less power than traditional LEDs. It is meant for small portable devices.

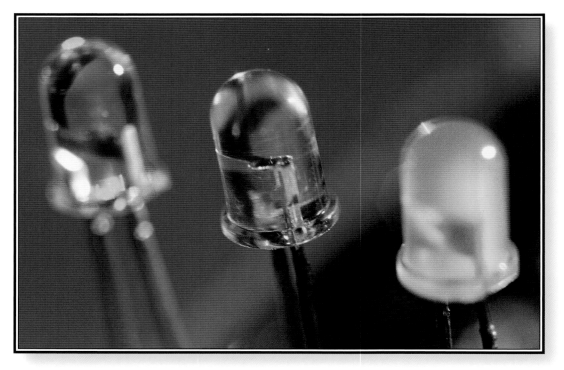

Light emitting diodes (LEDs) are used on many home appliances because of their bright colors and long lives.

Electricity Everywhere

Perhaps the most profound effect of Edison's light bulb was to inspire the electrification of the entire country. Entire large cities were wired for electricity very soon after the light bulb became available. Rural areas followed slowly.

The U.S. government helped spread electrification by establishing the Rural Electrification Administration (REA) in 1936. The REA provided loans for the construction of power plants in rural areas, thus improving the lives of country people. The agency was closed in 1994 because electric power was

Millions of light bulbs brighten New York City offices.

available in every part of the country. The REA power plants were then sold to private companies.

As the availability of electricity spread, new uses for it were quickly found. If you look around, many electric devices are clearly visible. For instance, along a city street, you will notice traffic lights. Without traffic lights human traffic controllers would be needed at every busy intersection.

Electricity runs air conditioners in summer. Many homes use electricity for heating in winter. Look around your own home. You will see refrigerators, stoves, washers and dryers, computers, TV sets, and radios. Don't forget to look around for small battery-operated devices. You will see TV remote controls, cell phones, cordless phones, clocks, and watches.

All these wonders of electricity came about because Thomas Edison needed an electric distribution system to operate his light bulb.

More Light Bulbs

Edison's success with his light bulb and his electric power companies made him very wealthy and increased his fame. One important improvement to the electric supply, however, was made by someone other than Edison. In fact, Edison opposed it. That improvement was the use of *alternating current (AC)* instead of Edison's choice, *direct current (DC)*.

Two Kinds of Electric Current

Edison's electric power plants delivered current to customers in the form of direct current. Edison opposed alternating current because he believed it was dangerous. Someone coming into contact with ordinary AC household electricity can be severely injured or even killed. He believed direct current to be far less dangerous.

Edison had a great sum of money invested in direct-current power stations. He insisted that his power plants supply only direct current. That created a major problem. Direct current at the low *voltage* needed by Edison could be transmitted only a short distance before it was lost. Many small power stations would be required to supply power to an entire city. Alternating current can be transmitted over long distances. One power station can supply many customers. Today electric power—alternating current—is transmitted over hundreds of miles. Edison's power companies faced a dilemma: use direct current or alternating current. They eventually chose alternating current. A former Edison employee, Nikola Tesla, showed the way.

Tesla's Solution

Nikola Tesla was an inventor and electrician who had once worked for Edison. He spent several years developing an electric motor that used alternating current. He also developed a power supply system to produce alternating current. He tried to interest Edison in his AC power supply, but Edison

Nikola Tesla's alternating current (AC) power supply was turned down by Thomas Edison, who preferred direct current (DC).

was committed to direct current. Tesla then turned to the Westinghouse Company.

It was Tesla's power system that interested the Westinghouse Company when they hired him, though he went on to make many inventions that are part of modern life. Westinghouse supplied its customers with alternating current and competed with Edison for the electric light business. After a time alternating current became the standard. That was a rare defeat for Edison. AC is still the standard used in the United States.

Once the incandescent bulb became widely used, other inventors and engineers began looking for ways to improve it. One early improvement was a filament made from the metal tungsten.

The Tungsten Filament

Tungsten was one of the metals Edison tested and rejected for his filament. He could not make the tungsten wire thin enough to be efficient. Instead, he first used carbonized paper and cotton thread. His most successful filament was made from strips of bamboo. The first bulbs using tungsten filaments were introduced in 1907. By that time inventors had learned how to make a thin tungsten wire.

In 1911 William Coolidge, working in the General Electric Research Laboratory, improved the very fragile tungsten filament by making it more durable. The tungsten filament was superior to Edison's because it lasted longer. General Electric followed that success by making a bulb that replaced its vacuum with a gas.

In 1913 General Electric introduced the gas-filled light bulb. The use of gas eliminated the need to create a vacuum in the bulb. At first nitrogen gas was used. Later argon gas was also used. Just as tungsten filaments extended the life of light bulbs, gas-filled bulbs have a longer life than vacuum-emptied bulbs. The gas bulbs are still in use today.

Fluorescent bulbs are more efficient than filament bulbs and produce white light.

The Fluorescent Bulb and Halogen Lamp

In 1939 a very different kind of light bulb was introduced. It was the *fluorescent bulb*. The fluorescent bulb was first displayed at the 1939 New York World's Fair. It was not presented as an alternative to Edison's incandescent lamp. It is completely different. It is rarely used in homes, except sometimes in kitchens, closets, garages, or workshops. It is mostly used in such public buildings as offices. The bulbs are long tubes and produce a bright white light.

During the late 1980s a modified form of the long fluorescent tube was developed. The new fluorescent tube is folded or coiled and fits easily into a lamp socket. This bulb is suitable for home use. These bulbs use less energy to produce the same light as an incandescent lamp.

THE FLUORESCENT LIGHT

Edmund Germer, the inventor of the fluorescent lamp, was born in 1901 in Berlin, Germany. After graduating from the University of Berlin in the 1920s, he devoted much of his career to inventing many lighting devices.

He developed the fluorescent lamp during the 1930s while working as a self-employed inventor. General Electric, the company founded by Thomas Edison, bought his fluorescent lamp invention.

Germer moved to the United States in 1951. During his long career, he patented twenty-two inventions in the United States and thirty in Germany. He was coinventor for many other patents. Germer died in 1987.

The *halogen lamp* was introduced in 1960. Halogen gas replaces other gases inside a lamp to produce a bright light. The nonglare properties have made the halogen lamp popular for automobile headlights.

The Light Bulb Today

If you visit a lighting store or even the light bulb section of a supermarket, you will find many different kinds of bulbs. There are the familiar 60- or 100-watt frosted bulbs that are used in your

The crystal ball used in Times Square in New York City on New Year's Eve uses six hundred halogen light bulbs, as well as ninety-six strobe lights.

lamps at home. You may notice bulbs shaped like candle flames designed to be used in chandeliers. There are large, heavy-duty bulbs for outdoor and motion-detector lighting. The long, tubular fluorescent bulbs that may be used in your kitchen or garage will be on display. You might want to examine the new compact fluorescent bulbs used in lamps. Some bulbs will be advertised as "long lasting," guaranteed to burn for several years instead of months. You will even see tiny bulbs for battery-operated flashlights.

Today, an assortment of light bulbs are available for various purposes, such as auto headlights for lighting roadways, flashlights for lighting a dark home, and LEDs to let you know your computer monitor is on.

All of these bulbs are simply improvements of Thomas Edison's original 1879 light bulb. That bulb was certainly his greatest invention, and he will always be remembered for it and the electric distribution system.

The Light Bulb: A Timeline

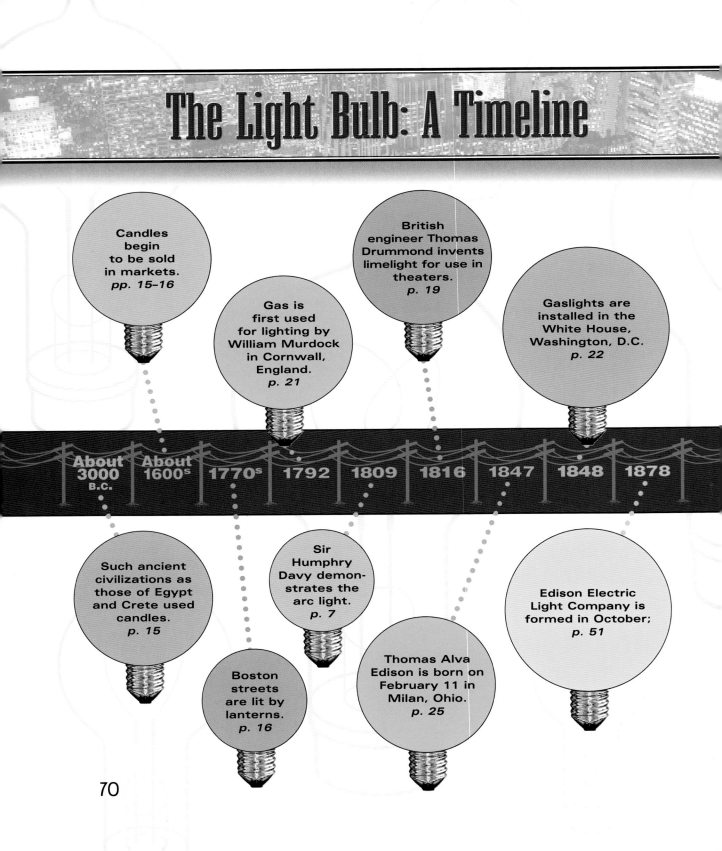

Candles begin to be sold in markets. *pp. 15–16*

Gas is first used for lighting by William Murdock in Cornwall, England. *p. 21*

British engineer Thomas Drummond invents limelight for use in theaters. *p. 19*

Gaslights are installed in the White House, Washington, D.C. *p. 22*

About 3000 B.C. | About 1600s | 1770s | 1792 | 1809 | 1816 | 1847 | 1848 | 1878

Such ancient civilizations as those of Egypt and Crete used candles. *p. 15*

Boston streets are lit by lanterns. *p. 16*

Sir Humphry Davy demonstrates the arc light. *p. 7*

Thomas Alva Edison is born on February 11 in Milan, Ohio. *p. 25*

Edison Electric Light Company is formed in October; *p. 51*

70

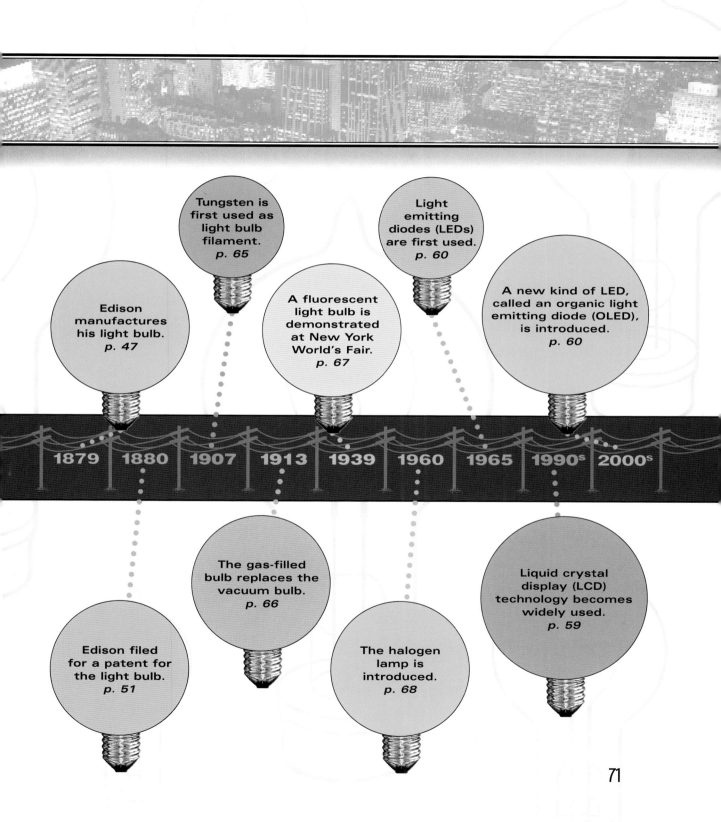

Tungsten is first used as light bulb filament. *p. 65*

Light emitting diodes (LEDs) are first used. *p. 60*

Edison manufactures his light bulb. *p. 47*

A fluorescent light bulb is demonstrated at New York World's Fair. *p. 67*

A new kind of LED, called an organic light emitting diode (OLED), is introduced. *p. 60*

1879 1880 1907 1913 1939 1960 1965 1990s 2000s

Edison filed for a patent for the light bulb. *p. 51*

The gas-filled bulb replaces the vacuum bulb. *p. 66*

The halogen lamp is introduced. *p. 68*

Liquid crystal display (LCD) technology becomes widely used. *p. 59*

71

Glossary

alternating current: Electric current that reverses direction at regular intervals; the standard electric current in North America

arc light: Light produced from an "arc" of electric current jumping from one wire to another

direct current: Electric current that flows in one direction only

filament: Wire inside a light bulb that produces light when heated by electricity

fluorescent bulb: Bulb that produces a bright white light

gaslight: Lighting device fueled by gas

generator: A machine for making electricity

halogen lamp: A lamp that uses halogen gas

incandescent: Glowing

kerosene: Fuel made from petroleum or coal

light emitting diode (LED): Light used to indicate whether an electrical device is on or off

liquid crystal display (LCD): Technology used for displays in notebook computers, digital watches, and other small appliances

pressure lamp: A lamp with an air pump for pressurizing fuel

stearin: Modified animal fat (tallow) used in making candles

torch light: A form of candle made by dipping rushes, which are grasslike plants, into melted fat

vacuum: When most of the air is removed from a container, a vacuum is formed; an emptiness of space

voltage: A measure of electric force; expressed in numbers of volts

To Find Out More

Books

Delano, Marie Ferguson. *Inventing the Future: A Photobiography of Thomas Alva Edison*. Washington, DC: National Geographic Society, 2002.

Price-Groff, Claire. *Thomas Alva Edison: Inventor and Entrepreneur (Great Life Stories)*. Danbury, CT: Franklin Watts, 2003.

St. George, Judith. *So You Want to Be an Inventor*. New York: Philomel, 2002.

Video

Edison: For All Mankind (video recording). Richardson, TX: Grace Products, 1998.

Web Sites

General Electric's Lighting Institute
http://www.gelighting.com/na/institute/aboutgel.html
A comprehensive guide to the history of lighting, including fun facts and a literature library.

74

Glenmont Museum

http://www.nps.gov/edis/edisonia/virtual%20tour/glenmont/glenmain.htm

History and virtual tour of Edison's New Jersey Glenmont Estate.

A History of Light and Lighting

http://www.mts.net/~william5/history/hol.htm

A chronology of light from the beginning of the universe to the present.

The Lighting Library

http://www.mts.net/~william5/library1.htm

Dozens of links to lighting Web sites.

Organizations

Thomas Alva Edison Memorial Tower and Menlo Park Museum
37 Christie Street
Edison, NJ 08820
732-549-3299
http://www.edisonnj.org/menlopark/museum.asp

Edison National Historic Site
Main Street and Lakeside Avenue
West Orange, NJ 07052
973-736-0551
http://www.nps.gov/edis/index.htm

IEEE (Electrical and Radio Engineers)
3 Park Avenue, 17th Floor
New York, NY
10016-5997
212-419-7900
http://www.ieee.org

Smithsonian National Museum of American History
14th Street and Constitution Avenue, NW
Washington, DC 20560
202-633-1000
http://americanhistory.si.edu/

Index

About the Author

John R. Matthews is a freelance author living in Abilene, Texas, where he writes nonfiction books for both adults and children. John has a masters degree in history from Tarleton State University, part of the Texas A&M system. He enjoys reading murder mysteries as well as history.

To research this book, John read several long biographies of Thomas A. Edison as well as numerous articles in encyclopedias. He was astonished at the many Internet sites devoted to Edison and his light bulb. Gazing at the insides of a (clear) light bulb, John was amazed that something so simple-looking was beyond the reach of scientists and inventors just a little over a century ago.